MY FAVORITE PETS

by Pearl Markovics

Consultant:
Beth Gambro
Reading Specialist
Yorkville, Illinois

Contents

My Favorite Pets............2

Key Words 16

Index.....................16

About the Author 16

New York, New York

My Favorite Pets

What do you love?

I love dogs.

They have wet noses.

I love goats.

They have soft fur.

I love birds.

They have colorful feathers.

I love cats.

They have long whiskers.

I love lizards.

They have green skin.

Key Words

birds

cats

dogs

goats

lizards

Index

birds 8–9   dogs 4–5   lizards 12–13
cats 10–11 goats 6–7

About the Author

Pearl Markovics has many favorite pets. She especially loves her black cat, Microbino.